Ministering to Millennials

The Challenges of Reaching

Generation "Why"

2nd Edition

Ministering to Millennials:
The Challenges of Reaching Generation "Why"
2nd Edition
By
Jonathan G. Pitts

Published by Greater Works Publishing
A Division of Greater Works Enterprises, LLC
www.greaterworksenterprises.com
2016

First Printing: 2014

ISBN 978-0-9975643-2-7

Greater Works Publishing
A Division of Greater Works Enterprises, LLC
Website:www.greaterworksenterprises.com

Dedication

To the Millennials

Grow into the people that God has purposed you to be.

Also Available From Jonathan G. Pitts

21st Century Sonship: Restoring the Art of
Apprenticeship

Heaven's Sound: Call to the Nations

Connect with Jonathan

Facebook: Jonathan Pitts
Twitter: @JonathanGPitts
Instagram: Jonathan_G_Pitts

The Millennial Journey Continues

Finishing this book is just the beginning.

Visit us at
www.facebook.com/MinisteringToMillennials
for more information, tips, and resources on reaching
the Millennial Generation.

Table of Contents

Introduction

Two years have passed since the first edition of Ministering to Millennials was published as a free eBook and since that time it has been downloaded in about 13 countries. I give God all of the glory, honor, and praise as He makes His Word known in the earth and His will known about the Millennial Generation. My wife Juarkena and I have had the opportunity to speak about the book and the topic of Millennials in different ways with the most noticeable being an invitation to appear on the Trinity Broadcasting Network (TBN) in January 2016. During the interview, we spoke on the many statistics that you will find on the following pages while also advocating for the need for the church to purposely engage this generation. One point that Juarkena made that speaks directly to the pulse of why we need to pay attention to this generation was this: The terrorist group known as ISIS that incessantly threatens the countries of the world has empowered Millennials on their side. Unfortunately, when you look at the demographic of those who carried out the recent bombing attacks in Paris, you will notice that they were Millennials. Her ultimate point being, in these cases, the passion of the Millennials that the Church should be directing and guiding is being perverted by our common spiritual enemy.

The Millennials are a passionate generation, but what, exactly, are they passionate about? They are passionate about purpose. I'll venture to tell you further that a Millennial who does not know his purpose in Christ should be one of the Church's primary concerns. The moment a member of Generation Y is disengaged from your preaching, from your pews, and from your programs, is the moment that you have lost him; not just to another church, but to an open door that could drag him down a slippery spiritual slope. You may wonder why this generation embraces Wicca, Atheism, and New Age thinking so rapidly. It's simply that the Body of Christ, in critical times, has failed to answer their simplest question: Why? Is it a wonder that this generation is shunning traditional marriage? They look to the Baby Boomers and Generation X asking "Why should I get married or support traditional marriage when it didn't work for you?" You may wonder why the Millennial is so quick to jump from job to job instead of sticking it out with one employer for 40 years. Simply because she may see more value in herself and wants to try something new; especially after seeing the company so quickly lay

> **A Millennial who does not know his purpose in Christ should be one of the Church's primary concerns.**

off people who gave up between 20 and 30 years of early mornings, late nights, tee-ball games, and family trips to achieve the company bottom line without so much as a 'Thank You' from management. So if it seems that Millennials are self-centered, well, they have a reason to be.

If you do a search for articles on Millennials and Money, you'll find a plethora of topics and titles specifically for this group. There some that even decry about the financial world the generation has inherited – From uncertain retirement to stock market and housing market crashes, Millennials have a reason to be a little shaky in their trust of the ways of the previous generations. As of 2016, the eldest of the generation is turning 35. Shouldn't this be the time of marriages, houses, cars, careers and children? A bit a research may show us that the 'American Dream' that pushed us into the college that gave us $100,000 of debt wasn't the glittering gold that previous generations enjoyed. Perhaps this scene is an allegoric example of what's happened in the church. Millennials were told 'this is the way to please God' and have grown to find it result in boring, stale, robotic rhetoric that has only left them relatively lifeless in spiritual matters. Would they love to have the Holy Ghost you brag about? Yes, but they also what to know what the Bible says about homosexuals without being given a side of fire and brimstone for asking. Don't you think they want to become a Pastor one day? Sure, but before they do, they'd like to know how to defend their faith rationally and intelligently without just saying 'You believe the Bible by faith' like a broken record.

You see, the Millennials are a special breed that, I believe, was purposely placed on this earth by our Lord. Why? To shake us up a bit. It will be this generation that will ask the church why they believe what they believe. It will be this generation that will refuse to follow the status quo without first getting an encounter with the God we so passionately believe in. It will be this generation that will demand the church operate in the anointing of Smith Wigglesworth and see a manifestation such as the Welsh Revival of 1904-1905. They want to see the power and will not be scared to demand that the church become who she was made to become – The Manifested Bride of Christ. Millennials are ready to see the Church walk in purity, holiness, and love without commanding the final judgement that is only reserved for the one sitting on the throne of

Heaven. This generation, Generation Y, if engaged, will bring a new and fresh fragrance and fire to the Church. It will be more than Social Media and new technological devices. It will be a group of human beings covered by the Blood of Jesus, forgiven of sins, filled with the love of Christ, and spreading the glory of God across the earth.

One thing we need to realize is that we are 20 years away from the Millennials being the next leaders in every realm of society. They are poised and positioned to be the next Presidents, Kings, Pastors, Senators, CEOs, and influencers that will determine how daily lives will be governed. Will we, as the Church, engage them now or try to change their minds as they sign possible legislation saying that the Bible is illegal? Body of Christ, it is our choice. It is up to us. I am reminded of Stephen in his speech to the religious leaders of his day in Acts chapter 7. Not only did he take the time to rehearse the history of the wonderful works of God for their ancestors, he also charged them and challenged them in the area of lacking sensitivity to see just who Jesus was and how important this visitation was to Israel. Even more so, he said specifically in verse 51 that they had always resisted the Holy Ghost. I pray that we are not the same. I pray that we take this opportunity as the Church to focus on the Millennials and make sure they know Christ for themselves. Why is this so important? Simply because Generation Z and subsequent generations are not far behind. They will look to the Millennials for the Christian foundation from which to build their beliefs. The decisions of today directly affect the generations of tomorrow.

Why Study the Millennials?

As of 2014, the Millennials, also known as Generation Y, make up the youth and young adult population. Generally agreed upon by researchers, the beginning birth year of the Millennial Generation is 1981 meaning that the eldest of this group is 33 to 34 years old. Without an official ending year to the generation as of this writing, the youth of this generation can be teenagers with the eldest being at least 18 years old. This generation is finishing high school, entering and exiting college, getting into the workforce, starting relationships, getting married, and may have young children. With that, there are some major differences that can be seen in this generation that should be both seen and addressed:

1) This generation is more technologically advanced than any other

2) This generation has grown in a world that allows them to immediately connect to any other person in the world at any time

3) This generation is defining and redefining the social and moral standards of the United States and the World

4) This generation is facing an extremely diverse group of contemporaries – Diverse in race, religion, and various orientations

5) Financially, this generation is in more debt than their predecessors

6) This generation is getting married and having children much later in life than previous generations

7) This generation is less likely to buy property and houses preferring to rent

8) This generation is not far removed from being the next set of leaders (social, political, spiritual, etc.) upon which the following generation will depend on for guidance

9) In this midst of all of these points, this generation is making a noticeable exodus from the church and Christian beliefs

Like the generations before them, the Millennials are at the tipping point of becoming the main source of worldwide influence in the world. The Silent Age (Born 1928 to 1945), The Baby Boomers (Born 1946 to 1964), and Generation X (Born 1965 to 1980) are preparing to see what kind of results their investments (or lack thereof) will bring forth in the Millennials and, subsequently, Generation Z. Of this group, over the next 20-30 years, will be the next Presidents, Kings,

> **The Millennials are at the tipping point of becoming the main source of worldwide influence in the world.**

Pastors, Politicians, Parents, Teachers, and Leaders. Why study the

Millennials? Because into their hands will be entrusted the resources of the world and the lives of the generations coming behind them. With so many questioning whether to trust the Christian God, become religious extremists, or determine that a spiritual world does not exist it would be wise to study what makes this generation tick and prepare for the decisions they may make in the years to come.

Who are the Millennials?

The Millennials (Generation Y) are the individuals whose birthdate begins in 1981 and any year afterward. According to the Pew Research Center there is not an official ending year to the Generation Y measurement although it is believed that the youngest in the range are in their teenage years [1]. According to the same report, the Millennials are leading in digital/technological trends, have lower income than the previous generations when they were the same age, are remaining unmarried (mainly due to the lower income and greater debt), are the most racially diverse generation in American history, are less likely to trust other people, and are optimistic about the future.

Douglas Main of LiveScience in his article "Who Are The Millennials?" [2] says:

> Millennials have been characterized in a number of different ways. On the negative side, they've been described as lazy, narcissistic and prone to jump from job to job . . . Other positive adjectives to describe them include confident, self-expressive, liberal, upbeat and receptive to new ideas and ways of living.

Generation Y seems to give the rest of the world the positive impression of being very flexible and willing to embrace change and new ideas. However, the negative aspects that the world seems to have of the generation is that of the millennial mindset being full of selfishness, lack of dedication, and overall laziness.

This generation is definitely driven when they can see the personal benefit behind endeavors but may struggle staying put or staying engaged when they are so used to being distracted and entertained by a constant stream of the new, the flashy, and the fashionable things in life. However, this generation is also extremely intelligent; they have inherited a world where all of the information they could ever need to make informed decisions is at their fingertips (and may be voice activated). Speaking to a 20-year-old in 2014 versus one in 1970 would yield us a completely different thought pattern, not necessarily because of the decade but because of the immediate access to information and facts. So, do previous generations see them as lazy because they truly are or could it be they value their time and they know that they can quickly prove whether a task could end up being a waste of their energy? Or are we dealing with a generation that is still looking for its identity beyond social media and digital connections? This generation could flip the government upside down with a few well-worded tweets but could lack the people skills to shake hands with a CEO and the soft skills to win over an offended friend.

Generation Y is flexible and willing to embrace new ideas but are also seen as selfish and lazy.

These and many other factors define the generation that will ultimately redefine how we see the world. The Millennials seem to want to change the world for the better by connecting to each other, collecting the most information, and creating the latest technology that will help them make their mark on the world for all generations to remember. . . without leaving the comfort of their couches.

The Generation That Asks "Why?"

From politics to parenthood and music to religion, Generation Y is not afraid to ask "Why?" One article says that "millennials have highly sensitive BS meters [3]." This generation is willing to step back and assess the performance of the previous generations and make educated decisions based on what has worked and not what everyone else says should be happening. Generation X and the Baby Boomers will tell a Millennial that he needs to go to college right after high school. The Millennial will then look at the previous generation and some of his contemporaries and notice the depth of debt that has been acquired by college students along with increasing amounts of graduates without jobs and ask "Why?" The same Millennial may be told by another older person to consider marriage and not to wait too late. The next question in the Millennial's mind ends up being, 'why would I get married when the divorce rate is over 50% in the USA and your marriage is one of those that failed?' Then a member of the Silent Generation speaks up and says "You're 27 years old and you need to get out of your parent's house and get your own place." The Millennial, with all due respect, then asks "Why? I already know that I don't make enough money to support a place to live. I'd like to move out but it would be wiser for me to stay with mom and dad until I save up enough money to move out and support myself in this unstable economy." The older person, who initially assumed that the Millennial was lazy, then thinks about how wise that sounds and allows him to continue with his Facebook post on his smartphone.

The same applies to those who take stages and try to connect with Generation Y. A politician may talk about getting out to vote for a new piece of legislation but failed to actually show how the new law affects the Millennial and, as a result, receives no response. The church preacher will say "Thus saith the Lord" but will miss the Millennial not because he doesn't respect God but because he has questions about religion, the benefits of tithing, same-sex marriage, and abortion that remain unanswered. When the Millennial asks "Why should I believe the Bible when it was written by men and could have been changed to force someone's agenda?" and

Generation Y is not afraid to ask "Why?"

he only gets "You believe the Bible by faith" instead of the theological reason for the Bible's strength the preacher loses the Millennial's mind and, as a result, his respect. The parents raising Millennials that have only said "Do it because I said so" when the teenage going-on college age child asks why will start to realize the disconnect only because the child cannot get a real answer when he feels there should be one by now.

Even teachers, scientists, and other established people and professionals should be aware that the Millennial is not one that is willing to just follow the current trends without a reason. After a while (even if they continue just to keep from rocking the boat) they will wonder and possibly ask "what is the point of this? Why do we need this information? How does it apply to me?"

Whether it comes down to morals, legislation, religion, science, or even recreation Generation Y will not remain leashed to a thought pattern willingly without the ability to understand why.

According to the Pew Research Center [1]:

Millennials are also the first in the modern era to have higher levels of student loan debt, poverty and unemployment, and lower levels of wealth and personal income than their two immediate predecessor generations (Gen Xers and Boomers) had at the same stage of their life cycles. . . However, the new generation of college graduates also have their own economic burdens. They are entering adulthood with record levels of student debt: Two-thirds of recent bachelor's degree recipients have outstanding student loans, with an average debt of about $27,000. Two decades ago, only half of recent graduates had college debt, and the average was $15,000.

Although Millennials may be able to get the jobs they ultimately desire and the income that could be comparable to the previous generations at the same age they seem to generally start their adult lives with a great amount of debt to pay off. In a time when there is access to more financial information and strategies than ever before it ends up being ironic that the technology-laced generation runs into economic struggles.

Les Christie of CNN Money [4] says that Millennials are not in a rush to buy a home and the result is a homeownership rate among young adults ages 18-34 that is brought to a new low of 13.2%. In addition, "Thanks to a sluggish job market, heavy student loan debts and tight lending standards, Millennials are moving out of their folks' homes at a snail's pace. In 2014, 31.1% of 18- to 34-year-olds lived with their parents, down slightly from 31.2% a year prior."

The Millennial financial struggle is both apparent and obvious. Whether the issue is lack of jobs, lack of education, or increasing debt Generation Y seems

Millennials face higher levels of debt, poverty, and unemployment than previous generations at their age.

to be feeling the economic crunch and it results in slower growth in all areas of life.

Marriage, one of the most historic and traditional institutions of mankind, and its relationship with the Millennials is waning to say the least. For a number of reasons, Generation Y is putting off marriage and it is a noticeable trend both visibly and statistically. According to Tami Luhby [5] "Today's young adults are on track have the lowest rates of marriage by age 40 compared to any previous generation. If the current pace continues, more than 30% of Millennial women will remain unmarried by age 40, nearly twice the share of their Gen X counterparts, according to a recent Urban Institute report." Unlike their predecessors, marriage is not seen as the starting point to life as much as it used to be. For Generation Y, priorities begin with education and finances. They understand that in the 2014 world that lack of education can lead to lower financial stability. Yet, ironically, as Millennials gain more education they find themselves in greater debt due to student loans and, as a result, remain financially unstable if they cannot find the jobs to support themselves, their homes, and their endeavors as singles. This is one factor that makes a Millennial choose to stay single longer.

However, according to Luhby "But the explosion in singles has its downsides. Married couples are often better off financially, which means they can spend more. 'The evidence shows that getting married increases wealth and income,' said Pamela Smock, a sociology professor at the University of Michigan." So, while singles are putting off marriage, they may actually be keeping themselves in a worse financial position by not getting married.

Amazingly, although the Millennials will not get married they will continue to co-habitate and have children out of wedlock. Pew Research Center [1] says:

Today's young adults are on track have the lowest rates of marriage by age 40 compared to any previous generation.

> Perhaps because of their slow journey to marriage, Millennials lead all generations in the share of out-of-wedlock births. In 2012, 47% of births to women in the Millennial generation were non-marital, compared with 21% among older women. . . Millennials join their elders in disapproving of this trend. About six-in-ten adults in all four generations say that more children being raised by a single parent is bad for society; this is the most negative evaluation by the public of any of the changes in family structure tested in the Pew Research survey.

With the advent of trends such as high divorce rates and same-sex marriage in the world previous generations may not be surprised that the Millennials are attempting to take the definition of love, life, dating, and marriage into their own hands.

When we think of the traditional rites of passage into adulthood we may think of graduations, moving out on our own, getting married, having children, home ownership, and getting jobs. However, this generation, more than any other, has taken these rites, redefined them, and, in some ways, has completely eradicated them.

Some former rites of passage into manhood were getting a job, getting out of your parents' house, getting married, and having children. The same for women where more of the pressure was on home-life choices related to getting married and having children. Though these major, personal achievement points may still exist they are definitely not given the same level of importance as they once had. According to the statistics previously shared, education and finance and the lack thereof puts all of the traditional rites on hold. Some of the rites, due to differing desires, have completely blurred the lines and destroyed the points of reference. Educational debt keeps the money from getting a job from actually allowing a person to move out from the parents' house. Same-sex relationships have removed the possibility of having children through natural means. Single parenthood (when unmarried) takes the child-rearing rite and puts it out of traditional order and causes economic and social strain according to the statistics.

Mr. Main [2] also states that this generation "has also been called the Peter Pan or Boomerang Generation because of the propensity of some to move back in with their parents, perhaps due to economic constraints, and a growing tendency to delay some of the typical adulthood rites of passage like marriage or starting a career." As a result of the combination of world circumstances and attempting to learn from the mistakes of previous generations (e.g. 25%-50% divorce rate in USA – Multiple sources disagree on the actual number), Millennials are deciding to stay put and think things through.

Should Millennials be held to the fire because of a slowness to embrace the rites of passage? It may just depend on the reasons. Laziness and fear can be combated but in the case of rightful reasoning, such as being in a bad financial state, as to why a Millennial won't marry then so be it. But what about those who may have the right reasoning but seem to throw away a moral code – e.g. those that won't marry for financial reasons but co-habitate and have children out of wedlock? Are they not setting themselves up on a spiritual slope that one can't help but to slide towards a horrible situation? Regardless of the spiritual implications, this is the reality of the choices that Generation Y is making based on the reasoning of the facts they've been given.

> **Generation Y has redefined and, in some cases, eradicated some of the traditional rites of passage.**

Millennials and Technology

I t goes without saying that technology and Millennials go hand-in-hand. The growth of technology and Generation Y's innate use of it actually define one of the major marks of the entire age range. It is also the very thing that separates them from other generations. Millennials "are 'digital natives'—the only generation for which these new technologies are not something they've had to adapt to. Not surprisingly, they are the most avid users. For example, 81% of Millennials are on Facebook, where their generation's median friend count is 250, far higher than that of older age groups (these digital generation gaps have narrowed somewhat in recent years)." [1]

With the vast majority of this generation technologically connected to the world, there is a great need to both understand the mediums by which they communicate and the devices they use to facilitate their lives. Whether it's a smartphone, tablet, or laptop, the constantly connected generation is able to reach across the world for information at a moment's notice. Of course, this can be both positive and negative and also opens the door for the need for people to not just know the technology but also how to socially operate with minimal human offense or embarrassment.

In an article entitled "How Your Social Media Profile Could Make or Break Your Next Job Opportunity" Lisa Quast [6] gives tips to social media users regarding how to keep a positive profile online. The reason being that employers take the time to search a potential candidate's online activity. If the candidate's activity is questionable then a job offer will not be given. The Millennial generation is a part of a time when seemingly harmless information that has been posted online can directly affect their lives and lifestyles.

Additionally, another article [7] says that "nearly 40 percent of Millennials believe losing their phone would have a bigger impact on their lives than losing their car." How drastically have things changed from one generation to the next where losing a phone could be seen as having a greater impact on someone's life than losing a car? Being constantly connected, Generation Y cannot imagine a life without the digital world. But with these advancements some are using

> **Growing up with technology is the factor that separates the Millennials from previous generations.**

their connectivity for good and for projects that will change the world positively. They are rallying support for community investment at home and abroad, starting businesses, innovating new ideas, and connecting with others to make a platform for fulfilling a cause [8].

If there are any Millennials without a technological connection, they are the exception and not the norm. The daily life of a member of this generation is going to consist of network connections, social media, and a completely digitized way of thinking.

The political views and leanings of the Millennial generation show a great mark of difference in the thought patterns of the previous generations. The Pew Research Center report [1] gives a detailed overview of the data provided from surveys on the stance of Generation Y. The vast majority (50%) of Millennials identify themselves as politically independent choosing not to officially side with either the Democratic or Republican parties. Those that do are mostly Democrat (27%) with some Republican (17%). However, support among Millennials to officially side and identify has been waning.

Regarding their political views beyond a solid party identification, majority of Generation Y leans democratic (50%) rather than conservative (38%). They support mainly liberal ideologies as shown through their stances on social issues such as same-sex marriage (68%) the legalization of marijuana (69%), and legalizing abortion (56%).

In contrast to the trends that seem to have grown more democratic, Larissa Faw, a Forbes.com contributor, points out in her article "How Millennials might save the Republican Party" [9] that "a growing number of millennials may start rethinking their Democratic viewpoints." One of the reasons being that the generation is growing up and starting families. As parents, Millennials have a different set of concerns relating to the protection of their children that were not there prior to parenthood. As the article mentions: ". . . millennial parents sharply become concerned about privacy. 29% of millennial parents say they 'use the internet less because of privacy concerns,' up from 9.8% of non-parent millennials who cut back on the Internet due to privacy concerns." In addition: "Millennials parents are also expressing more fundamental conservative values. Once millennials become parents those that identify themselves as 'conservative evangelical Christians' jumps from 9.6% among non-parents to 32.9% among parents, reports FutureCast."

This generation, just as any other, has one behavior pattern while young and single but may show a change in trends as they grow older, more mature, and begin to invest more into other areas of life such as family, careers, and desires for stable lifestyles.

Generation Y leans democratic and supports mainly liberal ideologies but grows more conservative as they become parents.

However, as of now, "young adults tend to be single and churchless — turning away from their predecessors' proclivity for religion and marriage, according the Pew Research Center survey. Almost two-thirds don't classify themselves as "a religious person." And when it comes to tying the knot: Only about 1 in 4 millennials is married. Almost half of baby boomers were married at that age. [10]" Millennials and their political stances will definitely be one to watch as they grow older and seek to define themselves further.

The relationship between Millennials and the Church seems to be shaky at best and has sparked great debate and discussion as to how to reach this generation and keep them engaged in ministerial lifestyles. It is such a noticeable area of concern that The Barna Group [11] states on their website that their work on their Millennials Project consisted of 10 years of research, interviews with 27,140 Millennials, and 206 studies. In addition, Rachel Evans' article entitled "Why Millennials are Leaving the Church" [3] speaks to her own experience in working with churches and speaking to the view that this generation has of the Christian faith. Perhaps the crux of the entire article that speaks to the issue at hand with the church and this generation is "What millennials really want from the church is not a change in style but a change in substance." Along with the statement "We're not leaving the church because we don't find the cool factor there; we're leaving the church because we don't find Jesus there."

Is it true that this age group is not seeing Jesus in the 21st Century church? What makes them think that churches are not doing the right things or worshipping Jesus to the point that his presence is readily available for all to enjoy?

Perhaps it comes down to how Christians and Christians Leaders are interacting with the real world the Millennials face on a daily basis and reacting to the information that is so readily available on their smartphones to challenge every principle that is preached with substantiated fact. Maybe they're looking for at least an acknowledgment that science is real, an admittance that there has to be more to address moral issues than quoting scriptures, and substantial understanding that saying homosexuality is wrong doesn't make the LGBT community disappear – some of whom may be friends and family of the Millennials in question.

They seem to have trouble believing that the same Jesus who walked the earth and lovingly died and rose again for all of the sins of mankind would send "representatives" who would stand at the funeral of homosexual person holding a sign that says "God Hates Gays." They get what the Bible says but they seem to miss the application of the factors of loving one's brother and looking at one's own life before judging another's.

"We're not leaving the church because we don't find the cool factor there; we're leaving the church because we don't find Jesus there."

The Barna Group's study entitled "Three Spiritual Journeys of Millennials" [12] says "Over half of Millennials with a Christian background (59%) have, at some point, dropped out of going to church after having gone regularly, and half have been significantly frustrated by their faith." Where does this large amount of dropping out come from? Maybe boredom or lack of relevant engagement. What about the frustration? What makes a person frustrated with the Christian faith? One commenter on Rachel Evans' article says "I've got no problem with Jesus, it's his fan club I can't stand!" In addition to this comment there are 9,863 more entries discussing the concepts of God, Jesus, and the reasons Millennials would leave the faith. Going further in the next chapters there has to be an understanding of the fact that this generation is not willing to waste their time hanging around in a place where it seems there is religion but no concept of reality beyond the four walls of the church.

Is the Millennial Worldview anywhere near a Biblical Worldview? With only 58% of them being absolutely certain that God exists [1] there may be a great divide in how this generation views the world versus the way the Bible shows us the world should be viewed. An article by Ethan Pope entitled "Developing a Biblical Worldview" [13] discusses that there are basically two worldviews, those that match God's worldview and those that remove God from the worldview. He argues that "Without a biblical understanding we have left ourselves open and vulnerable to adopting many of the false teaching and false systems of the world. Unless you know and understand the truth, anything sounds good and reasonable. Many a person has fallen for a lie, simply because they did not know the truth."

It would be necessary to know which way Millennials lean in their view of the issues in the world. For instance, who is Jesus to a Millennial? Is he mankind's savior, a great teacher, or even a figment of one's imagination based on a fairy tale? What about a moral code? Where does Generation Y go to determine what is right and wrong – the Bible, the government, or themselves?

Utilizing some entries from Ethan Pope's chart [13] in which there are three columns for the Area, the Biblical Worldview, and the Natural/Atheistic Worldview – there has been another column added with some Millennial notes to compare some of the generation's view to point out whether the majority would have a Biblical worldview.

Area	Biblical Worldview	Naturalism / Atheistic Worldview	Millennial Notes (Added)
God	There is a God	There is no God	Only 58% are certain that God exists [1]. Majority of Millennials may believe in only scientific explanations and evolution as the evident progression of how man came into existence
Creation	God created world as recorded in Genesis	World came from natural causes	
Man	God created man	Came into existence through millions of years of evolution	
Jesus	Son of God, Savior of the world.	Was a "good" man. Rejection of his miracles and teaching!	With only 58% being certain that there is a God [1], the amount of those who believe Jesus is the Savior of the world may be lower.
Moral Code	Given to us by God in Bible	Society has ability to develop best moral code, (or dictatorship, or opinion polls.)	Politically, the majority of Millennials are Independent but lean towards liberalism.
Tolerance	Live by Biblical Standard	Accept everyone and every system, (with exception of those with religious values)	With the majority of Millennials leaning liberal they would be more tolerant of all lifestyle choices.
Abortion	Life begins at conception and formed in womb by God. High value place on a life.	Since God did not create life, the value of life is less -- and can be disposed of.	56% of Millennials believe abortion should be legal in all or most cases [1].

Homosexuality	God intended for one man to be with one woman	Acceptance based upon cultural moral code and opinion polls	
Marriage	One man united with one woman.	Lives by no real moral code -- do whatever feels good, no accountability, self-serving, me focused.	68% of Millennials support Same-Sex Marriage [1].
Children	Life begins at conception, valuable to God, Asset to family unit.	Value begins after birth, Important to society	56% of Millennials believe abortion should be legal in all or most cases [1].
Heaven	Literal place where believers go for eternity	We make our own heaven here on earth. (No biblical heaven)	With only 58% being certain that there is a God [1], those who believe in Heaven and Hell as literal places and the Bible as God's true word would be a smaller subset.
Hell	Literal place where non-believers go for eternity	No literal hell. We can have hell here on earth.	
Bible	God's Word	Simply myth & legend	

Based on some of the major areas of Biblical discussion, the majority of the Millennial generation would follow a more atheistic worldview that does not include God and the Bible as their source for daily living and decision-making.

Understanding from the information presented thus far that the majority of Millennials are exiting or inactive in the Christian faith, are adopting more atheistic/man-focused thought patterns, and seem more frustrated with the church than any previous generation to date; how do we reach them? Beyond getting them born again through evangelistic outreach how do we reach them in the terms of keeping them engaged in the faith and reducing the numbers of those who feel that leaving the church is the option for them and their families? How they are reached starts with understanding who they are and what they care about.

Millennials are informed

First, there has to be the foundational understanding that this generation is more informed than any other generation . . . about everything. Why is this important? Because the moment that a Millennial can discredit the message or the messenger respect is lost. One study [14] reveals that 38% of Practicing Christian Millennials and 14% of all Millennials will use technology to search and verify something that was said from the pulpit. Each word that a Christian says as a representative of Christ cannot be idly thrown out because just as much information that a believer can have about the Bible there is just as much, if not more, out to discredit it. In an interview [15], renowned physicist and adamant atheist Stephen Hawking said "Before we understood science, it was natural to believe that God created the universe, but now science offers a more convincing explanation." So, what is a partial reason to actually study the Bible, Biblical History, and Theological information? The reason is that Millennials are not just listening to people and taking their words at face value. They are fact-checking and they are prepared to see if Christians can defend their faith.

Millennials are technologically savvy (they are digital natives)

Another area to make sure that Christians must understand the Millennial mind in order to be able to engage them intelligently is the area of technology. Majority of this generation is technologically savvy and their entire lives are connected to digital devices and mediums. A Christian who is unwilling to embrace the technology of the day is already light years behind being able to engage a Millennial. 70% of practicing Christian Millennials read Bible scriptures on smartphones or other devices while 34% of all Millennials check out a church, temple, or synagogue via a website [14]. If a least a third of all Millennials are using a church's website as a prerequisite for visiting how many churches lose out on winning a soul because they either do not have a website or their website is not up to par with the current advances associated with an organization's web presence? Also, we should not forget that 81% of Millennials are on Facebook [1]. So, just how many in this generation are not being engaged because Christians and Christian Leaders choose not to advance to where the new generation is living on a daily basis? Technology is here to stay. It will only get bigger, faster, and more engaging with content (Godly and ungodly); leaving out technology only leaves Generation Y unreachable to Christians.

Millennials care about what's going on in the real world

Although the general persona of the Millennial may seem as if he does not think about world issues, the statistics show the opposite. In 2008, Millennials came out in droves to vote in President Barack Obama; without whom he would not have won the Presidency [1]. They speak their minds regarding the sensitive issues of the day such as same-sex marriage and abortion legalization and they do not keep quiet when there is perceived injustice. In 2014, it was student protestors in Hong Kong who are crying with a loud voice for democracy in government [16] and the same youth who developed an app that

This generation is more informed than any other generation . . . about everything.

does not require cellular towers to communicate among each other [17]. The same passion applies in all countries with this generation when they feel as though justice has not been rightfully applied. Generation Y cares about the real world and the things that affect them and others. Christians would be wise to not disconnect from reality to only speak to spiritual matters. The Millennials want answers, even God's answers to the issues of the day that they and their families and friends are facing. Based on the statistics, this generation is probably the least likely to turn a blind eye to what is going on in the world to bury their heads in the sand of religion. God has an answer to all things and

Christians need to be ready to give it if they are going to reach this generation.

Ultimately, reaching Generation Y is all about being ready to address not just the individual, saying they are in sin and need a Savior. Truly reaching them will require wisdom that has an answer to the things they care about and the willingness to interact with them in the languages that they understand the best: those of technology and straightforward truth with answers to the question of "Why?"

The Barna Group gives 6 reasons why young Christians leave the church [18]:

1) Churches seem overprotective
2) Teens' and twentysomethings' experience of Christianity is shallow
3) Churches come across as antagonistic to science
4) Young Christians' church experiences related to sexuality are often simplistic, judgmental
5) They wrestle with the exclusive nature of Christianity
6) The church feels unfriendly to those who doubt

Christians would need to be prepared to express straightforward answers to these and other issues to retain the Millennial mind. According to these reasons, Millennials feel like Christians demonize everything outside of the church, church/faith is boring and irrelevant, churches are out of step with the scientific world, they are struggling to live up to the church's expectations of sexual purity in this culture, they are forced to choose between their friends and their faith, and they cannot express doubts about their faith. The thought pattern of this generation is one that is seeking answers and when they come up empty it seems to cause a disconnection, not just from the church, but from the Christian faith.

With all of the challenges presented, what does it take to keep Millennials in the church? Though not exhaustive, there are a few steps that Christians can take to keep this generation engaged and at the forefront for Christian beliefs.

1) Acknowledge and understand that they are Generation "Why?"

2) Constantly present Jesus and not gimmicks

3) Study to show yourself approved, a workman that does not need to be ashamed

4) Embrace their digital side

5) Apply the 5 Ways to Connect with Millennials

6) In the midst of judgment never forget grace

7) Hear them out

<u>Acknowledge and understand that they are Generation "Why?"</u>

As mentioned at the beginning of this study, the Millennials are not afraid to ask why. The foundational reasons being that they look around in their world and notice the actions of the previous generations. They have been taking the time to analyze what has worked and what has not. Coming to a Millennial with cliché answers and jargon may only leave them frustrated. They would prefer that a Christian says that they don't know the answer than to give out spiritual rhetoric. When they are understood in this area they may be more likely to not only respect the faith but also acknowledge and respect the God that can answer why even when humans cannot.

Constantly present Jesus and not gimmicks

To quote again the concern of Millennials as presented by Rachel Evans - "We're not leaving the church because we don't find the cool factor there; we're leaving the church because we don't find Jesus there." This telling statement should be a good eye opener to every Christian Leader. There is nothing wrong with presenting a beautiful building with well-organized staging and orderly services but to engage this generation they need to see Jesus. There is plenty of scriptural support for this challenge but the actions need to follow the revelations. The common denominator among all believers, new and old, is Jesus Christ. If we are not lifting his name, loving with his heart, preaching his words, and leading people to the cross that redeems then we can only expect embarrassment and disrespect from this generation.

Study to show yourself approved, a workman that does not need to be ashamed

This point from the scripture is made to apply to the fact that Millennials are checking up on the information coming from the pulpit. If a preacher says that money is the root of all evil and sees a Millennial roll his eyes, he should not be surprised to find that the listener did his research and found that it is the love of money that is the root of all evil and not money itself. Whether the subject is about death, Heaven, Satan, or love, the leaders need to be well versed in doctrine and theologically sound so that they both reach the Millennial and substantiate the points in the scriptures.

Embrace their digital side

If not the leader, there should be at least a group of dedicated individuals who are ready to tweet, share, like, and post to all they can about the goodness of God and the practical application of Christian principles. Recall the statistic that showed that about 34% of all Millennials check a church's website. Is your church's web presence the best it can be? Beyond the few church services that are held in a week what is going on in the rest of the 24-hour day that a viewer can see at any time on YouTube, Facebook, Twitter, or Instagram? Embrace Generation Y's digital side, find a way to interact with them in their realm, and keep them engaged.

Apply the 5 Ways to Connect with Millennials

The Barna Group has come up with 5 ways to connect with Millennials [19]. They are:

1) Make Room for Meaningful Relationships

2) Teach Cultural Discernment

3) Create Reverse Mentoring Opportunities

4) Teach Connection Between Vocation and Discipleship

5) Facilitate Connection with Jesus

Essentially, what we can gather from the article is that engaging Millennials requires showing them exactly how church and the Bible matters to their everyday lives. The meaningful relationships, when developed, bring Generation Y to a place of feeling like they are a part of the greater vision. Simply put, they need friends that attend the same church and serve in the same ministry. Cultural Discernment is

Acknowledge and understand that they are Generation "Why."

associated with taking biblical principles and revealing how God sees the world and situations that they face. Reverse Mentoring is a concept that is about cultivating their skills by not only having a person of wisdom oversee their progress but also gives the opportunity for them to be heard, to teach, to serve, and to spread their wings in their field or ministry of choice. The connection between vocation and discipleship allows Millennials to grasp how the Bible and spiritual matters apply to their work. They will show themselves to be more engaged to Christianity as they notice that biblical principles go beyond the walls of the church they attend. In facilitating a connection with Jesus, Generation Y must get to know the Lord for themselves. After all of the sermons, church work, and field trips, their engagement hinges on this major factor – Jesus Christ being the focal point of their hearts.

In the midst of judgment never forget grace

Millennials, just like any other generation, will fall, fail, and mess up time and time again. One of the most sensitive areas of this is sexuality. This generation, as presented in the studies, feel judged when they fall and the church does not feel like a place to come and talk about their real struggles. Many Christians and Christian Leaders often forget how they fell before God in the midst of their sin and pronounce judgment on the new generations. This generation, just like any other, needs the grace of God in the midst of their sin. Just as the Lord gave us individual grace every time that we fell in sin before Him, that same grace needs to be applied when ministering to the Millennials. When they feel His grace they will never forget it and their walk with God will continue.

Hear them out

Lastly, the generation wants to be heard. No matter what they may be feeling or how absurd it may appear to the previous generations, they want to be heard, understood, and treated like they matter. Whether it's a business idea or a new way to do ministry, the Millennials need to know that their input and ideas matter. They are willing to do everything they can to leave their mark on this world but the church needs to be willing to hear them with the ear of the Lord and believe that they will become what He created them to be.

Conclusion

Reaching the Millennial Generation should be a top priority. Not just because it is part of the Great Commission but they must be reached due to the fact that their decisions will directly affect the generations to come. With a growing worldview that leans towards atheism, it is up to Christians to determine whether the Jesus will be properly presented and represented in the world. The actions of today (or the lack thereof) will directly affect the numbers we see in the days to come. Will those who claim Christianity rise up, study, and present an uncompromising Gospel or will this generation grow more frustrated and turn further away from God? The decision is ours.

With the ultimate focus of this book being that of engaging the Millennials and understanding where they stand in relation to society and the church, it would benefit the Body of Christ to stay abreast of trends that affect the generation. In his article with Dr. Michael Hout, a Professor of Sociology at New York, David Masci records an interview asking why Millennials are less religious than older Americans [20]. While giving points such as generational differences and having a different mindset towards religion, perhaps the most interesting among the points given was an emphasis on the fact that Millennials' distrust for religious institutions can really be seen more in their distrust for all major institutions both religious and secular. The Q and A point was as follows:

Q: Is what we're seeing with Millennials part of a broader rejection of traditional institutions or is organized religion the only institution being affected?

A: Oh, it is widespread. It's just easier to quantify religious change because we have such good data on it. But Millennials' faith in nonreligious institutions also is weaker than they used to be. You see evidence of their lack of trust in the labor market, with government, in marriage and in other aspects of life. General Social Survey data on confidence in the leadership of major institutions show that younger people particularly are not as confident as older adults when it comes to institutions like the press, government and churches. But I think trust is not the whole story.

For one thing, there has been a long list of scandals in recent decades, such as Watergate, that have undone the reputations of major institutions the Greatest Generation trusted. Millennials didn't grow up trusting these institutions and then had that trust betrayed like older Americans might have. They didn't trust them to begin with. And these institutions have let people, particularly young people, down.

As we continue to look to the Millennials and take the time to understand where they are coming from with their thought patterns, we may be able to see why they have a tendency to shun what we know as church. The spark begins with a distrust of major entities that produce a level of control in the lives of people. Just imagine for a moment; this book has made the argument that Generation Y is Generation "Why" and has proposed that Millennials

Millennials don't just lack trust in religious institutions but all major institutions.

need to understand their purpose for performing an action or putting their trust in the hands of a church before they are fully engaged in the church's mission. If you were one who needed to know why or you already questioned entities that represented God, you may have trouble giving your all if you didn't have your questions answered. If you come to church and don't feel loved or you don't feel purpose, you, as an individual, could easily experience feelings of disconnection and eventually disdain if your voice isn't being heard. As a result, your view of church as a whole grows to be increasingly negative. Amazingly, the statistics reflected in another article [21] assist with this point. It turns out that only 55% of Millennials in the USA believe the churches have a positive impact on the country – Back in 2010, the percentage was 73%. Needless to say, a negative view of the Lord's church could eventually lead to a negative view of religion as a whole (while not necessarily having a negative view of God or Jesus).

So, where does that leave the Millennials as of 2016? Truthfully, beyond them getting older, their views of church, religion, and spirituality have not changed much and may have only grown worse as they determine whether they align with where church leadership stands on the issues of the day. One thing that definitely has not changed is the growing need for Millennials to hear and understand the fullness of the Gospel Truth. Yet, there is also a challenge to the Body of Christ and church leadership – they must take the time to really listen to Generation Y to understand what really concerns them and they must take the time to at least attempt to answer the many questions that they have of Christian Leaders and even the Christian Faith. Failure to do so could result in these number declining further. I pray that the Body of Christ would rise and reach this generation as they are in line to directly affect the spiritual condition of generations to come.

References

[1] Pew Research Center, March, 2014, "Millennials in Adulthood: Detached from Institutions, Networked with Friends"

[2] Main, Douglas. "Who are the Millennials?" (2013). Retrieved from http://www.livescience.com/38061-millennials-generation-y.html

[3] Evans, Rachel Held. "Why Millennials are leaving the Church." (2013). Retrieved from http://religion.blogs.cnn.com/2013/07/27/why-millennials-are-leaving-the-church/

[4] Christie, Les. "Millennials are staying put at mom and dad's place." (2014) Retrieved from http://money.cnn.com/2014/09/17/real_estate/millennials-still-home/index.html

[5] Luhby, Tami. "Millennials say no to marriage." (2014) Retrieved from http://money.cnn.com/2014/07/20/news/economy/millennials-marriage/index.html

[6] Quast, Lisa. "How your social media profile could make or break your next job opportunity." (2012). Retrieved from http://www.forbes.com/sites/lisaquast/2012/04/23/your-social-media-profile-could-make-or-break-your-next-job-opportunity/

[7] "Millennials and Technology." (2014). Retrieved from http://singlepoint.com/millennials-and-technology/

[8]   Jones, Allison. "Three ways Millennials are using technology to change the world." (2012). Retrieved from http://www.huffingtonpost.com/allison-jones/three-ways-millennials-ar_b_1904189.html

[9]   Faw, Larissa. "How Millennials might save the Republican Party." (2014). Retrieved from http://www.forbes.com/sites/larissafaw/2014/09/29/how-millennials-might-save-the-republican-party/

[10] Holland, Jesse. "Poll shows good news for Democrats with young voters." (2014). Retrieved from http://www.huffingtonpost.com/2014/03/07/millennials-democratic-party_n_4918445.html

[11] The Barna Group. "Barna: Millennials" Retrieved from https://www.barna.org/barna-update/millennials

[12] The Barna Group. "Three Spiritual Journeys of Millennials." (2013) Retrieved from https://www.barna.org/barna-update/millennials/612-three-spiritual-journeys-of-millennials

[13] Pope, Ethan. "Developing a Biblical Worldview." (2000). Retrieved from http://www.foundationsforliving.org/articles/foundation/worldview1.html

[14] The Barna Group. "How Technology is changing Millennial Faith." (2013). Retrieved from https://www.barna.org/barna-update/millennials/640-how-technology-is-changing-millennial-faith

[15] Lee, Rhodi. "Atheist Stephen Hawking denies existence of 'God': Science 'more convincing explanation' for universe." (2014). Retrieved from http://www.techtimes.com/articles/16687/20140930/atheist-stephen-hawking-denies-god-existence-science-more-convincing-explanation-for-universe.htm

[16] Hume, Tim; Mullen, Jethro; and McKirdy, Euan. "Huge crowds join Hong Kong protests on China's National Day." (2014) Retrieved from http://www.cnn.com/2014/10/01/world/asia/china-hong-kong-protests/index.html?hpt=hp_t2

[17] Riley, Charles. "This app is helping Hong Kong protesters organize without a cell network." (2014) Retrieved from http://money.cnn.com/2014/09/30/news/firechat-hong-kong-protest/index.html?iid=SF_T_River

[18] The Barna Group. "Six Reasons Young Christians Leave Church." (2011). Retrieved from https://www.barna.org/barna-update/teens-nextgen/528-six-reasons-young-christians-leave-church

[19] The Barna Group. "5 Ways to Connect with Millennials." (2014). Retrieved from https://www.barna.org/barna-update/millennials/682-5-ways-to-connect-with-millennials

[20] Masci, David. "Q&A: Why Millennials are less religious than older Americans." (2016). Retrieved from

http://www.pewresearch.org/fact-tank/2016/01/08/qa-why-millennials-are-less-religious-than-older-americans/

[21] Fingerhut, Hannah. "Millennials' views of news media, religious organizations grow more negative." (2016). Retrieved from http://www.pewresearch.org/fact-tank/2016/01/04/millennials-views-of-news-media-religious-organizations-grow-more-negative/

J onathan G. Pitts is a cutting-edge visionary who seeks to lead end-time generations to embrace their divine purposes. As an Entrepreneur, Author, Speaker, and Teacher, he is a thought-provoking developer of the mind who has the ultimate purpose of drawing people nearer to God and a greater understanding of Kingdom Principles. His gift as a Kingdom Builder provides life-giving blueprints from which the Body of Christ can emerge victorious in all areas of ministry.

Jonathan, is the Founder of Ignite Ministries through which he and his wife Juarkena minister and build God's people and develop them to reach their goals in ministry, marriage, parenthood, business, and more. He is also the Founder and CEO of Greater Works Enterprises, LLC., a business conglomerate offering services specializing in publishing, graphic design, and small business consulting. In addition, he is the Founder of The Greater Works Foundation, a non-profit organization that provides outreach to underprivileged, under-served, and underrepresented youth and communities by promoting financial literacy, educational enrichment, leadership skills, mentoring, and global service initiatives that will cultivate the next generation of responsible leaders thereby creating empowered citizens and communities.

Jonathan has appeared on the Trinity Broadcasting Network and is a sought-after ministry strategist providing wisdom and insight in a variety of areas. He is the author of several books and studies including:

- Ministering to Millennials: The Challenges of Reaching Generation "Why"
- 21st Century Sonship: Restoring the Art of Apprenticeship
- The Church Leader's Guide to Millennial Engagement
- Heaven's Sound: Call to the Nations
- And More!

He is the proud husband of Juarkena Pitts and the honored father of 3 wonderful children.

www.ingramcontent.com/pod-product-compliance
Lightning Source LLC
Chambersburg PA
CBHW031615040426
42452CB00006B/527